AS IT IS

Michael Greening

AS IT IS

Matador
9 De Montfort Mews
Leicester LE1 7FW, UK
Tel: (+44) 116 255 9311 / 9312
Email: books@troubador.co.uk
Web: www.troubador.co.uk/matador

ISBN 978-1906221-751

Line drawings by Sara O'Dwyer

Typeset in 14pt Times by Troubador Publishing Ltd, Leicester, UK
Printed in the UK by TJ International Ltd, Padstow, Cornwall

Matador is an imprint of Troubador Publishing Ltd

For my children – Tim, Jane, Marie-Ann and Sara

PREFACE

I am starting to write this to give me some clarity in my mind. Whether I am able to complete it, whether anyone will ever read it, or whether I am able to elucidate my understanding of life intelligibly enough for readers to follow me, I do not know. What follows has plagued me for over thirty-five years – at least half of my life – and as my time is getting in shorter supply, I know that it will be therapeutic for me to get this down on paper. I realise that most people will dismiss what I have to say because, in a way, it denies everything they accept as being a member of the human race. Yet, somewhere, there must be others who have reached the same conclusions as myself. I would love to meet them.

I should explain here, that I am as normal as most people who have been lucky enough to have been born and live in the comparatively civilised society that Britain has been during my lifespan. My life has therefore been easy and comfortable. My everyday existence must also mirror tens of thousands of others. I get out of bed in the morning, put on a dressing gown and slippers and make a cup of tea. Then I decide, or think I do, what I should do next. However that is my life on its normal or lower, day-to-day, plane. There is a higher plane that I enter the moment I reflect on what is really happening to me.

I have been continually surprised, since my mid-thirties, that I have never heard about or come across anyone else who appears to have reached the same simple - and to me blindingly obvious – conclusion. Yet that is so. I am conscious that some philosophers must have arrived at the same conviction as myself or, at least, considered it but - to date - I have not come across their writings. None of the science books I have perused or any general factual literature, that has come my way, appears to broach this subject. Perhaps this is a matter many intelligent people understand but dare not write about, because it would seem to trivialise all knowledge – and by that their own raison d´etre.

When I was a boy and later as a young man I often questioned what I had been taught, but these were usually peripheral matters. In the main I accepted the evolved wisdom of my elders and betters. We each have a completely individual set of circumstances that govern the way we reason. As I got older my way of thinking, by chance, gave me my own realisation that everything I had been taught and almost everything I had ever read or heard was – in essence – incorrect. Reality, for me, became completely different to the way in which everyone I knew accepted it. Most things were the complete opposite of whatever I had been taught. Cause and effect had been reversed.

Let me give some examples. I realised that politicians did not change society, I saw that they were merely reflections of that society. I understood that a supreme being had not created man, monotheists had created God in man's image. I accepted that many scientists had interesting things to say – but, so far, they invariably appeared to have missed the ultimate truth. I agreed that good and evil could be adjectives used to describe events – but knew that there was no such thing as a good or evil individual person. I had also become aware that relationships, supposedly between two people, were – in reality – only one-way situations.

These statements are rather sweeping and, if true, appear extremely bleak as they would seem to rubbish all human endeavour. For myself, I do not feel this is so. Humanity´s continual striving for fulfilment and happiness are all part and parcel of our normal plane of existence. I´m sure I enjoy living as much as any man. However I cannot escape from that higher plane of actuality. If I rationalise ´down´ - from the perspective of my own individual evolvement, or reason ´up´ - from the present scientific explanation for the evolution of all self-replicating life, including that of humans, I only arrive at the same - to me - rational conclusion.

However hard I wrestle with this enigma the same answer has always been given and my conviction has also been reinforced, without exception, with every single experience of my life since I first arrived at it. Briefly, this is simply that free will is a myth. Human self-determination cannot be logically possible.

I do not know if I will succeed but I will try to explain, as briefly as possible, how my thought processes arrived at this conclusion and I trust this may ring bells for some of you. Others may see flaws in my contentions and I would love to hear these.

To give a simple illustration of what I am suggesting, let us suppose that I am going by myself on a country walk - in an area that is new and unfamiliar to me. As I have no map, it seems unlikely that I will find a circular route. I expect I will proceed so far and then walk back again. It is a beautiful early summer day and I am strolling along a leafy lane between a wood and a field.

Coming round a bend, I find that the lane divides into two - a Y-junction at which there is no signpost. One of the paths is slightly uphill, leaving the wood behind, the other a little downhill keeping to the trees. Although very slightly different both routes look equally attractive.

I am usually impulsive so proceed in one direction without thinking of my options, alternatively I stop and eat the apple I have brought with me, while I 'consider' which route to take. You may perceive that I have a simple choice which, in any event, is of little importance. This is not so. I am only able to go to the left (or right) because of all the events in my life up to that moment in time - and my situation at that moment. Perhaps one route looks easier and I am feeling lazy - or I may prefer the challenge of the harder route. Perhaps I prefer to go uphill now as it will be downhill when I return. Perhaps I usually prefer woodland to open country, as it may give me the opportunity to see more bird-life. Perhaps, that day, I am in the mood for looking at views. Perhaps I usually instinctively turn left but, on this day, feel I should turn right to break that pattern. What I am attempting to explain is that, in reality, I have no option. Everything that has happened in my life before that moment will dictate what I do. If I stop to eat my apple - I may (or may not) go the other way as new factors are added to the dilemma. Of course it will probably not matter which way I go - either route could provide me with an enjoyable country walk. However there is a chance that the choice of one junction in the lane over another might alter my future entirely. If I go left I could meet a companion for life. If I go right I might be heading for an accidental death. Stopping to eat my apple may (or may not) have transformed or saved my life.

I am not a scientist, but my line of reasoning is based on pure logic not on science. However I will use some contemporary scientific knowledge, both mainstream and speculative, to help explain some of the observations I make. I am not a theologian, but I was brought up in a religious atmosphere and know that one great Hebrew philosopher came to a partly similar conclusion between twenty-two and twenty-three hundred years ago (orthodox Jewish scholars, who believe the wise man to have been King Solomon, place the text over 500 years earlier). Although often quoted by both Christians and Jews, they usually qualify his three words of wisdom in the first chapter of Ecclesiastes. "All is Vanity" is not a comfortable thought to carry around in your head.

You may question, that if there is no such thing as self-determination, how can I have ´decided´ to sit down and write this. The answer is in this short book and you will either accept it or dismiss it. As I write in my first paragraph, I have no idea if I will finish this. If I have done so it must be in print in front of you because that is – *AS IT IS*.

Chapter One

A VERY LONG TIME AGO

Astrophysicists calculate that our planet, The Earth, was formed about four thousand, five hundred and fifty million years ago. Paleobiologists generally agree that a thousand and fifty million years after its formation, the conditions on the surface of the Earth, its make up of chemical compounds – especially water, its temperature and its distance from its star allowed the first life forms to develop and flourish.

Although there are a number of theories, we do not yet know how life first originated. No scientist has so far been able to give a satisfactory explanation of how inert matter could transform itself into self-replicating organic molecules. A growing body of experts in this field suggest that life probably arrived here from outer-space, brought by chance on meteorites. This only moves the question. How did life emerge wherever it came from, in what is only known to us – at present – as an inorganic Universe.

If humanity survives long enough, perhaps we will find evidence of life outside the Earth, either inside our solar system or beyond. This may give us the answer.

The first life forms in our world were microscopic and aquatic. One of the earliest groups, of which fossils of their 'colonies' have been found, are know as Cyanobacteria. These single-cell organisms, which make their own food and are sometimes called 'blue-green algae', lived in the then largely oceanic Earth three and a half thousand million years ago. They still exist today. In the vast time scale of the cosmos it was as recent as five hundred and forty million years ago before larger organisms appeared. Many millions of years passed again before life found itself in ever shallowing seas and survived when the water dried up. The first terrestrial plants had arrived followed by the first land animals. We do not know who these first invaders were, however it seems possible that they may have been small crustaceans. When you next turn over some dead leaves in your garden give the woodlice some respect; they have been here for a very long time. Or possibly they were tiny semi-aquatic insects. The Class Insecta are the most diverse and resilient animals on Earth. The oldest land animal fossil so far discovered is that of a little millipede, which lived nearly four hundred and thirty million years ago.

If we again move forward in time, to three hundred and ninety million years ago, the land saw the emergence of the first Tetropods – or creatures with four legs. These were early amphibians, which spent part of their life in water and part on the land, and were the likely descendants of lobe-finned fish. Some amphibians evolved into reptiles and some of these were dinosaurs, a number of which became the largest land animals ever on the Earth. Some amphibians remained as amphibians, developing into new species and some others evolved into Amniotes, creatures resembling small lizards.

Some of these animals became more advanced reptiles with a few mammal-like features. We call these Synapsids and it is from them, over a period of about seventy million years of evolution, that the first mammals arrived on our planet.

The assumption of evolution is now the central idea of all biology. Although the system by which the theory operates was not suggested until the mid-nineteenth century, by Charles Darwin and Alfred Russell Wallace, the concept was thought and written about over fifty years earlier. This was notably by Jean-Baptiste Lamarck in France and by Darwin's grandfather, Erasmus Darwin, in England.

Charles Darwin and Wallace both arrived at the conclusion that biological evolution worked by the process of 'Natural Selection'. That is, as individuals of any species differed slightly because of small mutations between generations, those with the more favourable attributes – in relation to their ecosystems – would be the ones that would survive and reproduce more successfully than those individuals which were less favourable to their environments. Then, over time and as ecosystems changed, new subspecies and later new species would evolve. Unsuccessful lines became extinct. Although some of the explanations of Darwin and Wallace have required modification, and they knew nothing of the mechanism of genes and Deoxyribonucleic Acid(DNA), the main thrust of their theory is still accepted today.

One area where Darwin's ideas have been subsequently found to be incorrect is the pattern of evolution over time. Darwin saw the modifications, the changes, the extinctions and the emergence of new species as a continual process that proceeded at a steady rate. The fossil record reveals this not to be so. The history of life forms show that their diversification has always taken place in a very uneven way. Graphs plotting the arrival of new species or the departure of others will exhibit lots of crests and troughs. The highest peaks for new species took place after planet-wide catastrophes, that the scientists call 'extinction events'. Some of these were particularly devastating and are known in big-game hunting jargon as the 'Big Five'.

These events happened after big changes in the inorganic environment, due to temperature fluctuations and atmospheric transformations. Most were caused by internal factors on Earth, like the sharp rise in the carbon dioxide content of the air following periods of upsurge in volcanic activity. One at least, scientists have now generally agreed, was much more sudden and due to external forces.

Biologists who study the fossil record (Paleobiologists) tell us that the largest extinction event took place two hundred and fifty million years ago, when the majority of all life was wiped out. They have calculated that ninety per cent of both aquatic creatures and land plant varieties were lost at this time, together with about seventy per cent of land vertebrate species. This 'event' however took place over a number of millions of years. Following this, as volcanic activity on the Earth gradually calmed down, a period of very rapid growth in biodiversity occurred.

The most recent and most written about mass extinction took place sixty five million years ago. Only in fairly recent years has it become mainstream scientific opinion that this was caused by a massive meteorite, over twelve miles wide, that hit our planet – landing in the shallow waters of the present-day Gulf of Mexico, near the Yucatan peninsular. At that time the continents were of different shapes and in different places than today. North America was still joined to Europe and Asia. South of 'The Gulf of Mexico' there would have been a wide oceanic gap before reaching the South American land mass, that was then joined to Antarctica.

It is not easy to visualise the meteorite strike, but we can imagine that a world-wide nuclear war might have similar consequences. There would have been fire storms across complete continents and global dust clouds bringing everlasting winter and perpetual night. With a much depleted supply of dissolved oxygen most varieties of sea creatures perished. This included the ammonites, well known by their fossils today. On land there was a loss of many plant species and, among the animals never to return were, most notably, the dinosaurs. This time, however, the Earth would have started to recover within a few years. After the paradigm following previous extinction events, there was a new expansion of animal varieties to fill the emptied environments. On land new types of vegetation appeared and some of the small animals, that had lived in the dinosaurs shadows for millions of years, began to grow larger and diversify. These were the mammals, who were to become the new dominant species on Earth.

Another class of animal prospered well after the sixty-five million year ago disaster. This class today has almost twice as many species as the mammals. Every morning, armed with my cup of tea, I enjoy watching some of their colourful varieties from my kitchen window. These are the Aves, or birds, and it is now thought that they may have descended from small feathered dinosaurs.

The class of animals known as *Mammalia* have a number of defining characteristics. The most obvious one being the presence of mammary glands in females, which produce milk to feed their young. Early mammals would have laid eggs, and today there is a small archaic 'sub-class' which still do this. These are the four types of spiny anteaters, or Enchidas, and the Duck-billed Platapus. The platapus is only found in a few areas of Australia, enchidas are a little more widespread there and are also found in New Guinea. The main mammalian sub-class is divided into two groups which, since their emergence, have had separate lines of development. These are the Marsupials, which include the Kangaroos of Australia and the Opposums of North America, and the Placentals found throughout the world – on land and in the sea. Present day placental mammals range from the Blue Whale, the largest animal to have ever lived on our planet, to the Pygmy Shrew – one of the smallest placentals – and include Humans. Unlike the placental mammals, marsupials are born when in a very immature state within a few weeks of conception. The young then develop further in a skin pouch covering their mothers' mammary glands. There are some advantages – as well as disadvantages – of this way of giving birth and raising their offspring. It was originally thought that the first marsupials pre-dated placental mammals and were their ancestors. Now it is generally accepted that both groups evolved at about the same time.

Primates, from their title, have always been regarded as the most advanced and therefore the top 'Order' of the Mammals. One of their main features is to have five digits on their hands and feet and being able to grip objects with their hands. Many, but not all, primates also have opposable thumbs. However so do some other animals, including previously mentioned Opossums – which are marsupial. It is fascinating to appreciate that, although they have evolved down completely different lines, some marsupial and placental mammals – both having adapted to fit into similar ecosystems – have ended up looking very much alike. In addition to the Opossums' similarity with some lower primates, one of the best examples of this phenomena – known as 'convergent evolution' – is the Tasmanian Wolf (often known as the Tasmanian Tiger because of its striped back). The last recorded individual of this species sadly died in captivity on my first birthday, although some people believe there may still be a few alive in the wild today. This marsupial animal is in many ways similar to members of the placental dog family, its skull being practically indistinguishable from that of a Timber Wolf. This is one proof, if any were needed, of Darwin's theory.

In 1735 the Swedish naturalist Carl

Linnaeus, who was then in his late twenties, published the first classification of Animals, Plants and Minerals in a small book titled *'Systema Naturae'*. Although this predated Darwin's book on Natural Selection by well over a century, it is interesting to note that Linnaeus classified ourselves with the primates. When criticised by the church for this he wrote, that in the principles of Natural History he could find no difference between men and simians. The science of classification, usually known as Taxonomy, has undergone many changes since then. There are still many disputes today of where some extinct species, and even living ones, fit in on the evolutionary tree.

In Taxomony family trees, 'Orders' branch into 'Suborders', which then divide into 'Infraorders', which are further split into 'Parvorders'. The tree branches continue down further to 'Superfamilies', 'Families', 'Subfamilies', 'Genus', and finally 'Species'. Where possible I will avoid using scientific Latin names, as we proceed down the branches to the shoots on the end – but in some cases there is no easy alternative. In the same way as we regard primates as being the top Order of mammals, we can regard the *Haplorrhini* or 'dry-nosed' primates as the top Suborder of primates. Further down the tree, the Infraorder *Simiiformes* or simians – which include the monkeys, the apes and ourselves – are certainly the 'higher' primates. By the time we reach the Superfamily stage, the top group are the apes and their first biological Family are the 'Great Apes'. Here our relatives are down to Chimpanzees, Gorillas and Orang-utans. At the Genus stage we are on our own as *Homo sapiens* or man. In addition to ourselves the Homo sapiens genus also includes our 'cousins', the Neanderthals who were the first truly human people, and also our immediate ancestors from the past two million years – who were descended from 'proto-humans'.

At this point in my very shortened resume of biological evolution, we come to the Million Dollar question. Why are we 'light-years' ahead of all other creatures on Earth? We are certainly animals and have evolved by Natural Selection in the same way as all the others. Our ancestors were once small mammals who shared the earth with dinosaurs and their ancestors, like those of the dinosaurs, were small reptiles. These were descendents of amphibians, which evolved from bony fish – that today are the largest class of vertebrates on our planet. Vertebrates, however, only account for three per cent of all animal species. They are a tiny group of living creatures when compared with the insects and other Invertebrates.

I will not attempt to go further back into evolutionary history. There is still much debate about some of the earlier connections and the subject is a very complex one. Linnaeus regarded all life to consist of either plants or animals. In today's taxonomy, Fungi have been classified separately from plants (it is now thought that they are probably more closely related to animals) and new life kingdoms have been added. These are most notably *Protists*, which include some Algae, and *Prokaryotes*, which are made up of single-celled organisms like Bacteria and Archaea. What is generally agreed, however, is that all life evolved from a simple self-replicating organism about three and a half thousand million years ago. I hope to be able to answer the big question, of why man seems so much more advanced than other animals, in my next two chapters.

Chapter Two

TOWARDS PROTO-HUMANITY

The final stages of the evolution of man, from our most recent common ancestor with other apes, has been a subject that has kept me enthralled for very many years. The question of why we are so overwhelmingly different from all other living creatures – and how we arrived in this situation so comparatively quickly, would seem to be almost unanswerable. It is certainly not difficult to understand why most people historically and many still today, are of the opinion that a supreme being once created us.

Not so long in the past, human divergence

from the other Great Apes was thought to have taken place between twenty and fifty million years ago. This old estimate is now regarded as completely erroneous. It is currently assessed that as recently as ten million years ago we shared common descent with our three second cousins, the orang-utans, gorillas and chimpanzees. There are few DNA differences between orang-utans and ourselves, even less between us and the gorillas. The genetic difference with our nearest relative, the chimpanzee, is tiny and present evaluations conclude that our last common ancestor must have been living on Earth only three to seven million years ago.

There are two extant species of chimpanzees in the world today. The Common Chimpanzee, which is found throughout most of East, West and Central Africa, and the Bonobo, which is smaller, more gracile and only found in part of the Democratic Republic of Congo. The Bonobo, previously known as the Pygmy Chimpanzee, is a highly endangered species – with numbers now down to only a few thousand individuals. Very few early chimpanzee fossils have been found, so little is known of their recent evolution, however DNA studies would suggest that the two varieties split between one and two million years ago. It is interesting to note that, although the two species are very different in many ways, they have inter-bred. If their separation from each other is at the higher end of the proposed scale, this may be only two or three times longer than their divergence from man.

How is it then, if our nearest relatives and the two slightly more distant ones have so much in common, that we are so very different? The answer is twofold. First of all, there must have been some unique occurrence that occasioned the subtle biological differences between them and us. Second – that difference, which obviously gave us an enormous advantage, allowed a completely different type of evolution that was non-biological in nature to bring us to where we are today.

For our ancestors to get to that point in time – say five, six or seven million years ago – was already an enormous sequence of chance. The original metamorphosis that produced self-replicating organisms, the fact that the Earth was unlike all other known planets – both in its relationship with its star and its mostly oceanic surface, the survival of life at all through the extinction events, the accidental colonisation of land and the emergence of creatures with four limbs, the evolution of mammals and later their 'top of the class' primates, in gambling terms all these were many millions to one shots. It was almost like some young person winning the top prize in the National Lottery and then, by altering only one number per week, winning the top prize again – every week for the rest of their life.

The science of the emergence of man is now a very complex subject, with hundreds of specialised fields of study that would take many pages of this book to list. In the nineteenth century, the first 'human' scientists were often amateurs or semi-amateurs and simply termed themselves Naturalists. Today new specific scientific disciplines, some with long convoluted titles, seem to appear every month. Some eminent scientists, of course, have knowledge and expertise in more than one field. However, in the main, the experts fall into three different camps. These are the biologists – who study evolution from the molecular point of view, the palaeoanthropologists – who study the fossil remains of humans and proto-humans, and the archaeologists – who study the inorganic objects and constructions that man created and left behind.

The first camp, which only came into real prominence within the last fifty years, include people like Richard Dawkins – who holds the recently created 'Chair for the Public Understanding of Science' at Oxford University. He has popularised his findings and ideas with a series of very well received books expressing a 'gene-centric view of evolution'. As a non-scientist (and also a non-academic), some of the intricacies of his arguments elude me but I am prepared to accept that – fairly obviously – the actual mechanism of Darwin's theory can only be at the organic – biological level. The biologists, like all the other scientists, do not yet have all the answers and there is still much debate and disagreement between them. This is especially true in the field of linking mutations in genetic material – DNA and RNA (Ribonucleic Acid) – with a time scale.

Palaeoanthropology, a branch of

palaeontology (the study of all plant and animal fossils), has been going for a hundred and fifty years. It has produced a fascinating series of finds, interpretations and books about them. Although this helps us to understand what early humans and proto-humans may have looked like and gives us insights into how they lived – which the biologists are unable to provide – there is one serious shortcoming with this science. This, in simple terms, is the number of finds.

We can only speculate, but the average lifespan of early humans was probably about twenty years. In the case of proto-humans it would have been less than this. We can only also guess at population numbers and distribution. Although we originated in Africa, we know that successive migrations of proto-humans, archaic humans and modern humans expanded into other parts of the world – their movements governed by food sources and changing climatic conditions. Early humans would have only lived in family groups and global populations may not have been large. Many regional groups, that were too small and became isolated, would have perished.

However some continued and their numbers had to be large enough to sustain the genus. It is likely that there were a number of different species of proto-humans, and later early humans. We do not know at what point in time, the ones who were our direct ancestors remained the only survivors. Likewise it is possible that there were more than the two later 'sapiens' species, which we know about today. These were ourselves and our more robust cousins – the Neanderthals – who died out over twenty-five thousand years ago. Some fossils of particularly small early humans, found recently in south-east Asia, may have been a separate – now extinct – third species.

If we multiply an average of six generations per hundred years with, say, seventy thousand centuries, then multiply the answer times 'x' – being the mean world population of individuals during the seven million years – we will arrive at a figure of untold billions of 'people' who once lived. Yet Hominina fossil remains found so far, with dates prior to a pivotal event of about eighty thousand years ago (more about this later), only total in hundreds – with the significant ones numbering probably less than one hundred. Hominoid fossils are far rarer than the very occasional one-off death, which occurred in deep mud or other circumstances where the physical remains might have the possibility of preservation. Being able to find any of those few fossils is then mostly by chance. The overwhelming number of early humans and proto-humans that died – that is 99.999*(to a large number of decimal places) per cent – would have been eaten by carnivores and scavengers. Their remaining bones, if there were any, would have been blown to dust in the desert or savannah winds many millennia ago.

We do not know if any of the early proto-human fossil finds were of our direct ancestors, or the forebears of 'cousins' whose lines became extinct. For example – the Leakeys, a well known family of palaeoanthropologists, and their associates discovered a number of much-publicised fossils in the Great Rift Valley region of Kenya and Ethiopia. Yet there is no way of knowing if these are typical or not typical of the majority of the human-like animals who lived in their times. Biologists tell us that DNA samples, taken from a very wide range of ethnic groups in all corners of the world, would seem to indicate that everyone living on Earth now is descended from a single family group. They date that group – or perhaps a single female – not to millions of years, but to about one hundred and fifty thousand years before today.

The archaeologists may be able to tell us as much, if not more, about our ancestors than the fossil hunters. The Earth, or certain areas of it, is littered with man's early tools. Museums are full of them and if we look in the right place (in countries like Britain) with a little diligence we can find them ourselves. Early man would have used wooden and bone tools, but these have rarely endured. Many of those made of stone however – blades, hammers and arrow tips – look as new now as the day when they were in use. They range from the fairly crude to the highly sophisticated. Man is not the only mammal to use tools. The apes and some other primates frequently use then, as also do some birds – who certainly possess the intelligence of higher mammals.

Many scientists are still of the opinion that it was the use of stone tools – coupled with his emergence from the forest, with its arboreal and predominantly vegetarian way of life, that was man's catalyst. They conclude that man's change of habitat to the open savannahs of Africa, where they reckon he first became a scavenger and then a hunter with a more omnivorous diet, was enough to spark his emergence. I do not accept that scenario, which I suggest would have just produced a more intelligent type of chimpanzee. That is providing they had found ways to avoid the large feline predators of that day, after losing their ability to escape up trees. Proto-man needed something much more dramatic, he required a unique accident.

Chapter Three

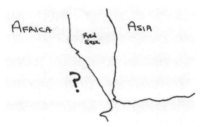

ARRIVAL OF MAN

Although it is difficult to see how there could be any – because no fossil corroboration has been found by the palaeoanthropologists, the main body of evolutionary scientists do not yet accept the following hypothesis. However a growing number go as far as saying that it is likely, and more accept that it is a possibility. The biologists may be able to come up with some validation but, as far as I am aware, this has not yet happened. To those who accept the theory and laymen – like myself – who read and think about it, the proposal seems so obvious that it is not easy for us to understand its current non-acceptance by the scientific majority.

For me the evidence, which is not from the past but is with us today, appears completely irrefutable. The traumatic environmental incident that set a small group of higher primates on the road that led to man – must have been water. A climatic or geological event in the area they inhabited, let in the sea and trapped them in a flood – which remained and in which they remained and survived. These were arboreal animals and initially the trees will have lingered, however within a few generations the forest, with the exception of remnants on small islands, would have dwindled away. The animals, who I feel certain were our ancestors, gradually adapted to their new home – which by good fortune they must not have had to share with dangerous reptiles. This sequence of events is usually known as the Aquatic Ape Hypothesis.

If you require the most glaring confirmation, before I go into any details, simply visit your nearest public swimming pool or – if one is not handy – stand in front of a full length mirror and take off all your clothes. What you will witness at the local baths – divers, swimmers, children splashing about – or in your mirror (whatever shape time has added to your body) is an extremely aqua-dynamic creature. To look at another species that are more so, you will need to visit the coast or a local zoo and watch the seals. It does not require much imagination to recognise that part of our ancestors later physical development must have been in water. Our nearest animal relatives, the chimpanzees and bonobos, have a basic body shape that is similar to ours – but they are quite obviously tree dwellers. Our bodies are far more streamlined. Everything about us, our nose shape, our hands and feet that can be used as paddles, our smooth skin and layer of fat under it – all are so suited for a water environment.

Standing upright on our rear limbs, assisted by the buoyancy the water gave us, caused our first divergence from the other apes. We became bi-pedal. We remained that way when the water finally dried up – again by chance. Being two-legged had its disadvantages, we were slower than most other animals and therefore would have been highly prone to predation. The advantages, to avoid extinction, needed to be substantial. One benefit was that our fore-limbs had become free so we were able to hold external objects for use as tools and weapons. Although important, this was not the most sensational adaptation that our return to the water gave us. That was a fortuitous by-product of two other associated changes.

Swimming in water, holding our breath when we were below the surface and our new posture of standing upright when in the shallows required adaptations to our breathing mechanism. To facilitate this, by chance and by natural selection we evolved modifications in the cartilage organ that controlled the air passage to the lungs. This resulted in giving us a lower larynx than that of other apes. The lucky side effect of this, was that we were able to make a much wider range of sounds than other species. We also, in common with other aquatic and semi-aquatic mammals, became consciously able to control our breathing. This made communications between individuals much more complex than is possible between other apes. It started the chain reaction of brain enlargement and more complexity. Before the water became shallower, proto-man had arrived. They had brains that were getting larger and as their brain size increased so did the sophistication of their communication.

All animals that have brains that encompass long term memories, are able to enter an additional phase of the evolutionary process. This is not biological in nature and, although it is governed by the same basic laws, operates in a slightly different way than the process of natural selection described by Darwin. This – learning by experience – is usually called *Cultural Evolution,* sometimes *Social Evolution* – when we are talking about the way groups evolve as distinct from individuals. With ourselves – Homo sapiens – it is this additional evolution that has brought us from our ape state to where we are today. Alone in the animal kingdom and, I feel certain, purely by the accident of our second aquatic experience, the wide range of vocalisations that our dropped larynx gave us – coupled with our new ability to breath in and out consciously rather than by reflex – developed into speech. Speech and our increasing brain size (helped, some say, by a mostly fish diet) set us on the highway.

Speech was the attribute that started to make us human and propelled us in a unique direction away from the rest of the animal kingdom. Beginning with warning calls, similar to those made by other primates, these articulations became more sophisticated and gradually – over many generations – developed into language. It was language that really made the difference, in leading us to our present state. Through language it was possible to communicate information and then knowledge from one individual to another and from one generation to the next. However, this was only part of the vast chasm that this ability established between ourselves and all other living creatures. It was from language that we evolved human consciousness. This was the genesis that 'created' us. I am of the opinion that possibly all animals, certainly all mammals (and birds) have a limited consciousness. What then makes human consciousness so different? I feel sure that the ability to think and reason, experience emotions, recall memories and everything else that our minds do – have all been constructed, shaped and enhanced by language.

Although it can vary widely with circumstances, verbal communication with other people may only take up a very limited portion of our waking hours. However we are continually talking silently to ourselves. For this we need language. I have little knowledge of the biochemistry of the brain but I suspect that the period of brain enlargement, that our proto-human ancestors passed through, was associated with the evolution of human consciousness. It must have been the self perpetuating cycle of more advanced language, increasingly complex consciousness and larger brain size that produced Homo sapiens. I understand that measurements have been made, and that our brain size has not not increased since 'modern' humans first appeared (the brains of Neanderthals were slightly larger). There is no way of knowing but perhaps it has reached its optimum size. It seems probable that our consciousness has also not been enhanced in the last ten thousand years – although our languages have become much more complex during this period. Perhaps the time for measurement is too short. Perhaps in a hundred thousand years from now (if we are still here) our brains may have expanded a little, as the evolution of language must surely be having some effect? Analogies may be a little wide of the mark, but a consciousness without language would be a little like the Internet composed entirely of pictures. Without any text, it would have no structure or form and there would be no index. There would be no way of finding whatever you were looking for.

When the water levels dropped and they were forced on to dry land again (they still lived, wherever possible, near the sea or lakes or rivers) our forebears had won the first prize in the lottery again and were at the peak of the evolutionary tree. They had large brains, walked upright and possessed rudimentary language. They were reasonably small, comparatively puny and slower than other animals that lived on the African savannahs. As such, they were very vulnerable as a food source for any of the fierce large carnivores of that day. There were probably not that many of them and they had to learn fast to avoid annihilation. Like some businessmen today, of small physical stature, who not infrequently out perform others – they had to 'apparently' overcompensate. Early proto-man, from being the most hunted animal, became the hunter. Rough estimates of time are not possible. How long the water period lasted and how long ago they left it, are unanswered questions at present. Yet we know that within the last million years ex-aquatic ape has conquered the Earth. He has become the controller – so he thinks – of his own destiny.

Although the idea was first suggested in the 1950s by eminent Marine Biologist, Sir Alister Hardy, the Aquatic Ape Hypothesis has been largely popularised over the last thirty-five years by a series of books written by Elaine Morgan. Elaine is not a scientist, so it may be partly for that reason that what she has put together has not been accepted as mainstream evolutionary thinking. However many scientists have collaborated with her and what she has written makes sound sense. Previously a highly successful television playwright and scriptwriter, her books are easy to read and – if looking at yourself naked in the mirror doesn't convince you – her arguments are likely to. I had a short correspondence with Elaine in the early 1990s and we met once in Oxford. She is a small unassuming Welsh lady, now rather elderly, so her account of how man became man is unlikely to take centre stage in her lifetime. Elaine would prefer to say how woman became woman. It was strong feminist views which first engendered her interest in the subject. Tired of the male-dominated descriptions of the evolutionary story that had been written before her own, she titled her first book *'The Descent of Woman'* (published 1972).

There are many aquatic and semi-aquatic mammals today plus a few, like ourselves and including elephants (who have been known to swim over fifty miles in the sea), who spent part of their later evolution in water before becoming dry-landers again. We have features in common with all of them. It is true that none of them talk or live in cities, but then – we were the only ones that were already at the top of the primate tree before we had the aquatic experience. In addition to the ability to consciously hold our breath (which is a pre-requisite of speech) necessary for all mammals that have to dive under water (not possible in all the others that don't), we have also developed an unconscious mechanism that slows down the heart beat when under water. This adaptation is only found in aquatic and semi-aquatic mammals. Again this very divergent group of many species all have little or no hair/fur and a thick layer of fat under the skin. The only non-aquatic mammals who have this fat encumbrance, are those who build it up for part of the year only – prior to hibernation.

Another possible sea water connection with humans, not found in other apes, is the production of saline tears. This phenomenon can also be observed in present day aquatic mammals (and oceanic birds) as a method of expelling excess salt from the body. Did it once have the same function in our ancestors? The list of our aquatic ties is endless – and there are some peripheral observations that may or may not be associated with our water period. In her earlier books (less seriously scientific than her final one), Elaine Morgan suggests that the evolutionary basis for a woman's strong and long head hair (the only ape with this), may well have been an adaptation for babies and young children to hang on to when in the water. It is definitely true that newly born babies are very much at home in water. The aqua-birth proponents are almost certainly correct in their assertion that this is the most natural way for both mother and infant. Apparently aquatic mammals (including whales and dolphins who have been back in the water for seventy million years) all engage in the act of coitus face to face. This is another human trait (until the plethora of 'recreational sex' manuals of the last half-century encouraged experimentation).

The Aquatic Ape theorists do not know where this period in our evolutionary history took place. It would have been in Africa and one suggested site is the below sea level depression in the present day Danakil Desert, near the border between Ethiopia and Eritrea. This site is also adjacent to the narrows between the southern end of the Red Sea and the Gulf of Aden – where some evolutionary scientists feel certain was the place where the first Homo sapiens emigrants crossed from Africa to today's Yemen. From where they colonised the rest of the world. It is unlikely that we will ever know for certain, as it would seem rather unlikely for any tangible evidence from that period to have survived and be recognisable.

There may, of course, have been more than one place and more than one population. Groups could have left the water earlier or later – or both – than the one group that survived extinction and from which we are all descended. Palaeoanthropologists generally agree, that there was more than one and probably a number of species of proto-humans. However we have no idea of how many or have any clue of the numbers of individuals in any of those populations at any one time. It seems certain that there were earlier hominid species and probably later ones than ours, which also left northeast Africa. Extinction was the fate of all of these, in some other part of the world. Others remained in Africa and became extinct there.

For a long time I have enjoyed an interest in family history. This is a subject that is generally confined to the last five hundred years, being the main period for which written records (in the UK) still exist. As every genealogist is aware – when compiling family trees – there is no predictable pattern in descent. Some successful and wealthy Victorian families, of many sons, have already completely vanished – within a few generations. Whereas another of – say – a mother with a single sickly child, perhaps resident in a work-house, has flourished within the same period into a small tribe. So it was with our ancient ancestors. If the evolutionary biologists are correct – in their estimation of one hundred and fifty thousand years ago – for the date when a family lived on Earth who were the forebears of us all, I am of the opinion that that family – in turn – must have been descended from one of the families that lived in the water. All the countless millions of other lines of descent came to dead ends.

The main purpose of this book is not to re-tell our evolutionary story – I use it only to clarify how we arrived where we are. I therefore make no apologies for my personal assertion that our ancestors temporary return to water makes sense. My conviction is always reinforced, when I am taking a shower or sitting in the bath! Elaine Morgan is much more modest and accepts that, until there is some tangible proof from the past, alternative evolution scenarios have as much validity as the one she writes about. In her final book she changed the original term *Aquatic Ape Thesis,* used in her earlier writing, to the amorphous but more scientifically correct *A A Hypothesis.* Personally I feel sure that AAH will become mainstream science in time. Its growing number of advocates include the most well-known television naturalist, Sir David Attenborough.

Whether or not what I have written is substantially correct, my contentions remain equally valid. The one word that crops up, at every stage of the history of life and our place in it, is chance. Evolution by natural selection cannot ever set out to achieve goals, it can only react to circumstances that have happened or are happening. The mutations that drive the process occur quite randomly and the ecosystems of all other living species, in each and every particular environment, can again only be altered by chance. The environments themselves are also changed by completely un-foreseeable haphazard events in the inorganic world. Without chance there can be no change. Without chance the Earth would have remained in the same inorganic state as when it was first formed.

As humans we are 'locked-in' to the

evolutionary process, in exactly the same way as every other living organism. We did not 'decide' to become people any more than grass decided it would become grass. Evolving the facility to be consciously able to hold our breath, which enabled us to dive and swim under water – and gave us the accidental by-product of speech, were not 'decisions' that we made. They arrived purely by natural selection. Man, as a species – like every other species, can only be changed by what already has happened and by external accidental events. As speech – and much later writing (and today probably the Internet) – has given our cultural evolution its ever-accelerating momentum, some people believe we have left and are now above the animal kingdom. They are in error. We are still animals – and beyond that living organisms, only able to adjust to what has happened to us and what is happening to us at this moment in time. The next moment in time always has been – and still remains – beyond our control.

Chapter Four

INDIVIDUAL EVOLVEMENT

At the start of this reflection, I used the adverbs 'up' and 'down' with the words evolution and evolvement – to differentiate between our arrival here as the human species and the individual growth of each one of us. That is our personal development from the moment of our conception until the current point in time – when I write or you read this paragraph. I will continue to do this, although both words mean the same thing and are – indeed – part of the same process.

The word evolution has been used, in my last three chapters, to describe the sequence of events that followed the chance chemical process that produced microscopic organic life here on Earth. This occurred about three and a half thousand million years ago or, maybe earlier, somewhere else in the Universe. I have given an extremely short summary of that process – through tiny aquatic organisms to fish – to four-limbed land animals, through to mammals and primates and our current biological state as Homo sapiens. There are, of course, hundreds of books on this subject. Most of them are written by professionals in their various fields or by other capable writers. All of them will give you a more complete understanding of that long and complex process, than this sketchy account. At the end of this reflection, I list some of the books that I have read and that have therefore influenced me. There will have been others and I apologise to the authors for their omission. I have also used the word evolution to cover the most recent period in the history of our species. This being the epoch during which our immediate ancestors changed in a non-biological way and diffused throughout our planet. This period culminated in the social explosion that started about ten thousand years ago, when the alterations in our forebears' cultural world began to escalate. This was fuelled by the rapid increase in the exchange of experience and knowledge after some of them gave up their previous family-group, hunter-gatherer existences to live in more settled tribal communities.

Individually, each one of us has also been changed – since the moment of our conception. I would now like to consider our evolvement.

On the fifteenth of August 1769 an Italian woman, born as Maria Ramolino, gave birth to a second son – in a family of eight children – on an island in the Mediterranean. A number of Moslem children were certainly born in Baghdad on the twelfth of February 1258. The capital of present day Iraq was, at that time, one of the most heavily populated and important cities in the world – a centre of learning, with an intellectual civilisation reaching back thousands of years. On the fifteenth of August 1998 Avril Monaghan, expectant with twins and already the mother of four other children under seven, went shopping in her local town in the United Kingdom. Accompanying her were her youngest child, eighteen month-old daughter Maura, and her mother Mary. On the twelfth of February 1809 an impoverished farmers wife, born Nancy Hanks, gave birth to her second child in a small one-room log cabin in Kentucky USA.

Some of these selected dates coincide and they all concern the birth or imminent birth of children. Although they have been picked at random, from the countless billions of incidents in reported world history, we must agree that they are all governed entirely by accident or chance. The island in the Mediterranean was Corsica that, although it was a British 'Protectorate' for short periods before and after the date in question, was French when the baby was born. By a chance of history his birthplace had been ceded to France, under the first Treaty of Versailles, in the year preceding his arrival. If the regional political dates surrounding his birthday had been just a little different, he might have been a citizen of the Italian Republic of Genoa – like his parents. Alternatively he may have been British and so eligible to join the British Army. As it happened he became a French soldier. Today Napoleon Bonaparte is regarded as possibly the greatest military tactician of all time and the premier architect of present-day Europe.

The twins, due to be born at some time after August fifteenth 1998, were sadly never to arrive as citizens of the world. They were blown up with their mother, little baby sister and their grandmother – by a bomb planted by the 'Real' Irish Republican Army in Omagh town centre on that date. The babies born in Baghdad on twelfth February 1258 did live but only for a few hours or days. Estimates vary but some historians reckon that up to one million people* – almost all the inhabitants of the city and surrounding areas, men, women and children – were butchered after the city was sacked on the thirteenth of February and during the week that followed. The largest Mongol army ever assembled, under Hulagu Khan – the grandson of Ghengis, carried out this massacre. Life in Baghdad is very precarious in 2007 – when I write this. There was no life at all – for the citizens of that then rich and highly civilised city in 1258.

The baby born in Kentucky on the twelfth of February in 1809 did not die. However he suffered many early childhood privations, as his parents lost their log cabin – and for a period of time the family was obliged to live in an earth dugout. Although he met his death from an assassin's bullet his life was a remarkable one. Abraham Lincoln is remembered today as probably America's greatest President.

I could give many millions of examples of the timely or untimely birth of well-known people in history. Illustrations of the people we do not know because their lives were never recorded are without number. Most of us will accept that the circumstances of our birth are a complete lottery. Prior to our arrival here, our conception is an even greater gamble. The union of a particular sperm with a particular egg – and the chance of that union – has very long odds and is completely unpredictable. If conception takes place, the resultant embryo will have had no choice in its parents or their antecedents. Its sex, its race and physical features, its inherited robustness or weakness, its intelligence or even the statistical chance of a long or short life – should it develop and endure until birth – are all imponderables.

It is pointless to talk about survival

percentages, but most of us can agree that to be born at all must be a complete accident. Who we are at birth must also be seen, by most of us, as the overriding controlling influence of our life. So far – at least – we should all accept that free will has not come into the equation. I would guess that that the majority of us would accept that the same must be true for the early years of our childhoods. Human babies are completely helpless for a comparatively long period of time. Their life is entirely in the hands of their mother and/or other older humans. The circumstances into which they are born, the location, the year and time of year, will all have a greater or lesser impact. Fairly obviously – the child born to a mother, who is a member of a nomadic tribe in a drought prone area of Africa, must have a different expectation of life and lifestyle to that of the offspring of an affluent, middle class couple in Europe or America.

If the child does survive until the age of four or five, when I suspect that many of you may think that free will can then be taken into account, its influence would be so small that it would be surely immeasurable. Perhaps you are of the opinion that self-determination only kicks in at a later stage, when a child becomes a teenager or a young adult? If we think long and hard enough about this, some of us may realise that it can never be so. The same rules that govern our physical evolution as a species must still apply to our personal cultural evolvement as individuals. We can only change by the random selection of events that have already happened, in our lives and before our birth, coupled with other events that may be happening at that point in time. There is no possible way we are ever able to determine what may happen.

I wrote a little earlier that cultural evolution works in a slightly different way than organic evolution. Jean-Baptiste Lamark, the Frenchman who was one of the first people to seriously consider evolutionary theory, thought that there was a mechanism of over-compensation that drove physical change. Darwin and Wallace – and all the scientists who followed them up to the present day point out that this is not possible. Natural Selection can only derive from what has happened or is happening. Of course there can be unexpected by-products of the changes – which may look like over-compensation. The by-product of speech that made us human must be the best example. Another would be the evolution of feathers on some dinosaurs, selected naturally as part of a way to control body temperature, that have now given their descendants the ability of flight. Cultural evolution can be simply described as the evolvement of non-physical ideas. Although some people may think that Lamark's suggestions may have some validity here, I'm sure the same Natural Selection rules still apply. The difference is purely speed – and with speed the ever-increasing production of by-products. This has driven us from our bronze-age existence of four thousand years ago to the technological complexity we live in today.

As a species we have been here for a very short time. People, who looked like some of us today, only emerged in Europe less than 45,000 years ago. They would have been descended from an earlier anatomically modern Homo sapiens species, who evolved in Africa about four times longer ago than that. Our Neanderthal cousins arrived in Europe and Eurasia about 130,000 years ago and our joint ancestors perhaps a quarter of a million years before then. Dragonflies, some much larger but others almost identical to the varieties with us today, were flying around and catching weaker insects over three hundred million years ago. The marked increase in our numbers, with its accompanying acceleration of our cultural change, appears to have occurred in the last ten thousand years. The start of this coincided with the retreat of glaciations at the end of the last Ice Age. Yet, as far as we are aware, we are still in the Ice Age cycle and the ice is likely to return. This may be after a particularly warm period that many, but far from all, scientists are predicting we are currently entering. Whether or not these present climatic changes are mainly or partly a by-product of man's increasing activity on Earth is in dispute. What is not in dispute is that we are completely in the hands of our inorganic environment. If a meteorite, only a little larger than the one that landed in the Gulf of Mexico to end the age of the dinosaurs, hit the Earth by unlikely accident after you read this – it is more than probable that the human species would not survive.

HISTORICAL NOTE: For a quarter of a millennium before 1258, Baghdad had been the most populated city on Earth. In the Eleventh Century it had become probably the first metropolis with over one million inhabitants. By contrast London, which in the late Nineteenth Century became the first place in the world with over five million citizens, was quite small in 1258. At that time England's capital would have been home to less than fifty-thousand souls – and this figure was to be halved a hundred years later, following the arrival of the Black Death.

Chapter Five

POLITICS and BUSINESS

If individuals are unable to make 'decisions' that are in any way not governed entirely by their past, up to that moment in time, coupled with their interaction with everything outside themselves at that moment – what is the relevance of politicians, generals, business tycoons, media proprietors, managers, teachers, parents or anyone else whose main purpose in life would appear to be to direct and control other individuals. The answer must be no relevance – apart from being part of the rich tapestry of life and living.

Politicians are useful, in that they provide (in our 'Western' civilisation) a fair proportion of the stories, comments, analysis and occasional scandal without which some newspapers and newscasts would have difficulty in filling their pages and time. They are unable to alter anything, however, outside the general evolution of the society in which they operate. It makes no difference if they have been elected, appointed by others or self-appointed. They are only reflections of that particular society at that point in time. They have as much impact on everyone's lives as an ever-running television soap opera. They can be as interesting, amusing or incredibly boring and we are able to watch and listen to them or completely ignore them. If we go away for a holiday, they will still be there when we return. We may (or may not) 'switch' them back on – and hardly realise that we have missed a few episodes. Like the soap opera, they do not and will not actually change our lives any more than every other inter-action outside ourselves.

Western-style 'democracies', where there is a judicial system independent of the apparent ruling political group, are generally the most stable and therefore frequently the most pleasant and preferable states in which to live.

They are, of course, not all alike and I am only able to write about Britain – where I have lived for most of my life. This country has been described by some people, especially those who were born and brought up elsewhere but now reside here, as one of – if not the most – civilised countries on Earth in the present day. I might feel otherwise if my home was in a city but living – as I do – in a very rural and beautiful part of this land, it is easy to agree with that description. The reason for this has nothing to do with politicians, but everything to do with geography. Britain's 'civilisation' depends on an extremely complex structure of influences, with an intricate web of checks and balances. These have evolved, many of them comparatively peacefully, over centuries of time. The fact that this occurred on an island, of about the right size just north west of continental Europe, is by far the principal factor. However, the forces of equilibrium are still precariously balanced. Even here, we can see that it is far from impossible – at some future date – for an unpredictable event or series of events to plunge the country into anarchy and chaos.

Politicians, although part of the process, do not control it. Like all other evolvement, political change can only follow what has happened before – adjusted by external events at that time. Momentous changes in political history, like the 1790 Act that substituted hanging for women convicted of certain crimes – in place of being burnt alive at the stake, could not have been agreed by Parliament at an earlier date. The abolition of the slave trade in 1807, would not have commanded a majority poll the previous year. The Suffragette movement could not have persuaded the House of Commons to grant women the vote before the end of the First World War in 1918 (not all women until 1928). Nor could the very recent power sharing arrangement in Northern Ireland, or the smoking bans in Wales and England, have started at any time before the year in which I write this.

Individual politicians have all arrived where they are by chance. Many of us, when small children, seek applause and praise and are apt to show-off in front of our parents and other adults. The thespian ability that may evolve from this can assist in future careers.

This is especially so if we end up in show business, as barristers, confidence tricksters, salesmen, clergymen or politicians (when a word ends in '-men', this includes the ladies as well). A number may try two or more of these occupations. A few children dream of going into politics. For some of these, their future is as predictable as an undertaker's offspring following his father into the family firm. Prime Ministers William Pitt, Robert Peel, Stanley Baldwin and Winston Churchill are good examples of such sons. Others may be brought up in families where political ideas are common subjects for discussion, between their parents and their parents' friends, so the catalyst can be discovered there. A smaller number arrive seemingly accidently, after unlikely events. Few people, for example, would have predicted that John Major would reach high political office. What may have happened if he had not been turned down for a job as a bus conductor – or if the family business of manufacturing garden gnomes had not failed? Although he had entered local government years earlier, it may have been the chance situation at his bank employers – where he was made an assistant to a director who had been previously the Chancellor of the Exchequer – that furnished one of the early steps in his meteoric rise.

Success in business is as unpredictable as reaching the top in politics. Often someone who has achieved great material prosperity, starting a business from scratch in the garden shed and reaching a position – when still comparatively young – of having an army of employees and many millions in the bank, will say to a group of young hopefuls – 'you too can do this'. They will point out all that was required, in their case, was a good idea plus lots of hard work. Some budding entrepreneurs have silly or impractical notions that are bound to fail, but others do have clever and original business plans that look like winners. Some of these innovators then work day and night, putting all the effort they are able to muster into turning their conceptions into reality. Yet prosperity eludes them. Making a lot of money, the most obvious measure for business success, has always followed a combination of chances taken and chance. Individuals who are unable to take chances will rarely get anywhere. The maxim about speculation and accumulation almost always rings true. However the main ingredient is external chance.

Chance is everything, we cannot will the future or foretell it. It would have been as impossible to see what life had in store for the little baby boy, born in 1889 at a little village in Austria – to the third wife of a man who had changed his name from Schicklgruber, as it was for the little Albanian girl born twenty-one years later – in the town that has now become the capital of the Republic of Macedonia. In common with a fair proportion of other children, the little boy suffered an unhappy childhood under a domineering and sadistic father. He and his sister Paula were also the only two of six brothers and sisters to reach maturity. Yet these were only two factors out of countless thousands that shaped the boy's early life. We have been told that as a young man he would have liked to have been an artist but, because of circumstances and by chance only, he entered the history books as the man responsible for fifty million untimely deaths. It was simply chance that he survived rather than one of his other siblings. It was simply by chance that Hitler became Chancellor of Germany in 1933 and that World War Two followed a few years later. We can only speculate if Hitler might have been taken less seriously, had his father not changed their surname (schickl can mean smart but grube translates as pothole). Although individuals appear at the pivots of history, in reality they are like the single hair that tips the scales. If they had not been there, another hair would have been likely to produce a similar if not quite the same outcome. In other words, if Hitler had died as a child it is more than probable that the second world war and everything associated with it may still have occurred. We would just have different names in the books. On the other hand, of course, it may not.

The little girl born in 1910 was one of many who had a happy childhood, although her father died when she was eight. By the age of twelve she had decided to become a nun, leaving home six years later never to see her mother or sister again. She first travelled to a convent in Ireland, to learn English, and from there the following year to India – where she remained for the rest of her life. In 2003, only six years after her death, she was beatified by Pope John Paul II as Blessed Teresa of Calcutta. Today the 'Missionaries of Charity' order she founded, to help the destitute and outcast members of society, has over 4,000 nuns and many more lay helpers worldwide. Yet Mother Teresa's legacy, like Hitler's, resulted from uncountable numbers of random events.

Famous military commanders, from the past, have often been political leaders as well. As the apparent architects of history, ordinary mortals like me used to mentally file them in one of two boxes. We were taught as youngsters to regard them in the same way as the cartoon cowboys of childrens' television. They were either 'white-hats' or 'black-hats', very few of them were grey. Today's teaching has changed – certainly for adults. A small number from Nero to Hitler – and now joined by others like Pol Pot – are likely to remain permanently black, but many have been re-listed or have joined the greys – awaiting reclassification.

The wild Central Asian black-hats of my

childhood, like Genghis Khan, Tamerlaine and Babur are now regarded as civilising intellectuals rather than cruel barbarians. Although I could never fully understand why they were blacks. Presumably this was because they did their conquering by travelling West. Alexander the Great, who lived a similar lifestyle, was always a white-hat – but he conquered in the opposite direction. The East European terrorist, Attila the Hun, is another now wearing light headgear. He had already changed in my mind, after seeing him portrayed by Jack Palance in a 1950s movie. If you travel to Uzbekistan today, all Lenin's and Stalin's statues have been removed and replaced by those of Timur (Tamerlaine) – now their greatest national hero. Similarly in South Africa, Shaka – who also had a lot of blood on his hands and (despite Rider Haggard) used to be regarded as a black-hat – has given his name to a new international airport. He is now revered as the founder of the Zulu nation by former friend and foe alike. A few hats have changed the other way. When I was young I was told that Henry Morton Stanley's patron, King Leopold the second of Belgium, was responsible for opening up heathen central Africa to the Christian missionaries and the benefits of civilisation. He is now portrayed as having been a particularly nasty individual – with a very dark hat indeed. Stalin, now considered to be responsible for even more misery than Hitler, was reported in the newspapers of my youth as dear old 'Uncle Joe'. Mao Zedong, whose portrait was worshipped in family altars only thirty years ago, has now been omitted from Chinese school textbooks.

All these names in the history books were creatures of their period, circumstances and chance. They were all, in reality, always as hatless as the day when they were born. There were and are no villains or saints, we are all subject to the times in which we live. Internationally, the most famous Englishman who ever breathed is usually recognised as the boy born in a small midland market town nearly four hundred and fifty years ago. By chance, his prime years coincided with the age of the first Queen Elizabeth – and the blossoming of the theatre in London. If he had been born and had arrived in the capital a few decades earlier, he would not have found any amphitheatres or playhouses. Shakespeare, the greatest word-smith in the English language, would still have been a great poet but there could have been no plays.

Chapter Six

OURSELVES IN THE UNIVERSE

Although the millennium started with great expectations for my wife and I, by the spring it had turned into a year of fear and sorrow. My dear Flemish companion of forty-two years – and the mother of my four children – was diagnosed with an inoperable cancer. The initial search for treatment and the later acceptance of fate were difficult times for both of us. My wife died in early September and I understood, for the first time, why grief is such a very different word from sadness. My wife was a Christian – and I spoke of her and her life at the church funeral service. It was while I was preparing the words I needed to say, that I suddenly became aware of the circumstance when the very first Homo sapiens animals became truly culturally human. This must surely have occurred when some small family group carried out the first deliberate burial. We will never know what led up to this incident, but we may be able to visualise the scene. The dead individual was possibly a child but may have been a mother, a mate or the senior member of the group. This was also, very likely, the point in time when the concept of religion was created; the moment the idea of some existence beyond the grave took root.

These first inhumers of their dead – so the original psychological humans – were not our direct ancestors, but an earlier species we call Neanderthals. One of the first fossilised remains of these people had been discovered in the Neander valley, near Dusseldorf in Germany in 1856, from where their title derives. Only a few years ago, some scientists were of the opinion that people today might have some Neanderthal ancestry (it was suggested that red hair might be one of their genetic characteristics). However, more recent biological studies seem to indicate that this is not so. As our direct ancestor – Cro-Magnon man (named after a rock shelter in France) – co-existed with Neanderthals for some thousands of years in parts of Europe and Eurasia, it would have been very strange indeed if there had been no inter-breeding. The fossil hunters have found the remains of at least one individual with features from both species. If the biologists are correct, this can only mean that all the inter-bred lines died out.

The dates of the first burials are in dispute. Although Homo sapiens remains, as distant as over 200,000 years old, have been found after excavation in caves these were likely to have been accidental internments. The first ritualised burials, where flower pollen or simple grave goods have been found with the remains, date from about 80,000 years before now. Many burial sites probably await discovery, so earlier dates could be confirmed in the future.

Man is not quite unique in his respect for the departed. Many animals appear to mourn the demise of a companion and ape mothers have been known to carry around the body of a dead infant for hours and occasionally days. Elephants, of all the animals, seem to have feelings with the greatest similarity to man – which could be described as emotion. They frequently cover the body of a deceased family member with leaves and branches and – even years later – may return to where the bleached bones lie to pay homage to them. I have seen a group of elephants myself, in South Africa, standing in a circle around some bones and raising their trunks in unison – as if in reverence.

Several important utilitarian deviations began to separate our Homo sapiens but pre-human forebears from all other species of animal, in addition to their ability to speak. Although the use of tools is now thought to even pre-date our evolutionary split with the ancestors of chimpanzees, those utilised by the bi-pedal branch gradually became far more sophisticated. The biggest divergence occurred when the fear of fire was overcome and its control mastered. This chance discovery almost certainly saved our kind from predacious extermination and goes back at least one and a half million years. Finding out that fire made meat much easier to eat would have been a much later revelation. The earliest 'hearth' that has been identified dates from rather less than half a million years before now. It has recently been suggested that as human body-lice evolved from smaller hair-lice about one hundred and fifteen thousand years ago, this could indicate the epoch when the first animal skins were used to help keep us warm. Coinciding with these advances, scientists have found a number of instances – both with Neanderthals and our direct ancestors – where the remains of individuals show that they had been severely injured or incapacitated by disease some years before death. This can only mean that there were strong human-like bonds between family or clan members. It shows that those who were fit must have helped others less able to survive. Although this trait can also be observed in some other animals, Homo sapiens is the only species where this apparent altruism continued for long periods of time.

Becoming human was not something that happened in an instant, but a gradual process that took place over countless generations. However, if a moment in time needs to be given, the very first deliberate internment of a deceased family member must be the special day our ancestors stepped above and away from the rest of the animal kingdom. You may wonder where all this is leading and what proposition I am attempting to make. I am suggesting that it would seem likely that we, in our present biological state as *Homo sapiens sapiens* – following a little after the Neanderthals (*Homo sapiens neanderthalensis*), only became fully cognitive human beings within the last eighty thousand (or a little longer) years. Although rudimentary language had evolved long before, prior to the first burials we were just the brightest and most advanced animals around.

Although these first humans' social evolution followed a variety of patterns in unconnected parts of the world, a marked change occurred about ten thousand years ago. This was especially so in areas of the Northern Hemisphere, where the retreat of the last great glaciation caused a rise in sea levels. The warmer temperatures made life a little easier and lifespans a little longer. With the resultant increase in population, some humans started to live in tribes rather than family groups. Two or three thousand years later these coalesced into the earliest embryo civilisations, assisted by the discovery of agriculture and – in more than one place – the first picture writing. These primitive societies would have also been held together by the birth of community 'religious' rituals. Then, from about five thousand years before now, our cultural evolution slotted into top gear. This accelerated at an ever-increasing pace until first printing, over five hundred years ago, followed by the industrial revolution two and a half centuries later sent it into over-drive.

In my lifetime there have been many in-depth studies of a wide range of animal species, which has revolutionised our understanding of them. The mindless dumb animal conception, held by most people in Darwin's day a century and a half ago, has been replaced by the realisation that they are not so very dissimilar to us in very many ways. They do not have language but many of them have complex communication systems. Some also appear to have telepathic powers which we may have once also possessed, but have now lost. The notion that Homo sapiens is the only 'conscious' species, with emotions, has also been partially dispelled. So, although in a sense, we waved goodbye to the rest of the animal kingdom on that day – eighty or more thousand years ago – when we felt such empathy for a deceased member of our species that we buried them (we also started to bury our pet dogs from about 17,000 years ago) – we never really left them. We are biological animals – with large brains and language. The rest is just layer upon layer of clothing and accessories.

Not only are we animals but we are also living organisms. We still have much in common with all the rest of the biological world – with plants, fungi, bacteria and everything else that is not inert matter. This being so, the only thing that separates us from every other form of life is evolution itself. Evolution can only be pushed from behind. It can only take account of what has happened and is happening. Free will may be an idea but it is illogical. If it is absurd for bacteria, grass, woodlice or rabbits – so it is also for us. It is not possible.

My earliest realisation that I was not able to 'determine' any of my actions came, I guess, when I began to accept that relationships between individuals were not as most of us assume them to be. Even the apparent strong bonds between many couples, children and parents, family members and lifelong friends – were not quite what they seem. Every one of us is many different people, not only at separate stages of our lives but at the same time. The person we are to our partner may be quite dissimilar to the person we appear to be to our parents. We are other people again in the eyes and minds of our children, to other members of our family, our friends, our work colleagues, our boss or our employees, our casual acquaintances – or to complete strangers. We are also very different people to ourselves – whether we are looking in the mirror or not. Which one of these people then are we; are we all of them or none of them?

A few months before I write this, judicial authorities in Iraq decided to end the life of their former president – Sadam Hussein. Here in Britain, and also in America, we were informed by most of the media that we were well rid of a ruthless dictator and enemy of our country – although a few decades ago, when his army was battling with his eastern neighbours, the same

media told us he was an ally. To many people –
for instance most Palestinians – he was a hero.
To some of his own countrymen he appeared
extremely evil and cruel, while others
worshipped him. To some people close to him he
was clever and intelligent, to others vain and a
fool. His children – when they were young –
knew him as a loving father, his wife as an
honourable husband and his grandchildren
looked up to him as their idol. To some people
he was honest and a man of his word yet to
others he was devious and a liar. To himself, no
doubt, he considered he was many things and
perhaps – towards the end – misunderstood. But
who was he? He was – as we all are – many
contrasting people. We only really exist in the
diverse, and often completely contradictory,
perceptions of others – and in our own, usually
rose-tinted, opinion of ourselves. There is no
single you or me. Our conceptions of our parents
and our children change considerably as we all
get older, as they may over time with a partner,
wife or husband. Love is a word we use when
the awareness is benign between both parties at
the same time. It doesn't work quite so well
when it is one-sided. We do not – in fact – 'love'

another person. What we love is our own perception of that person, in our own mind, at that point in time.

I'm sure that it was from this realisation, engendered by my quest to understand my relationship with my wife, that I began to understand the illogicality of free will. Although I regard myself (and others tell me they do) as a particularly impulsive person, that adjective really has no meaning. If we think about it enough (that, in itself, is something we may or may not be able to do) we can realise that any action we take, or thought we think, or emotion that engulfs us can only possibly be derived from everything inside ourselves – accumulated up to that instant in time – coupled with everything external to us but influencing us at that moment.

We are all aware that when we look into the night sky we are looking into the past. This is the simplest way to understand our own insignificance. With the naked eye it is possible to look beyond the billions of stars in our own Milky Way and see our 'near' galaxy neighbour, Andromeda. Depending how measurements are taken, this galaxy (official name *Messier 31*) is larger than our own and contains about one trillion stars. A trillion has twelve noughts. As this galaxy is over two and a half million light years away from us, the light we see – without the aid of a telescope, left there probably not so very long after our ancestors had diverged from those of the chimpanzees. However there are galaxies one hundred times more massive than Andromeda. Some, that can be detected with instruments, are so far away that light left them – not only before life here but before the Earth itself existed.

Some of the estimated one hundred billion stars in our own galaxy dwarf our own Sun. One has been found, in the far reaches of the Milky Way, that is calculated to be forty million times brighter than our star. As there are billions of galaxies out there all containing billions of stars, the mind cannot conceive the infinite numbers involved – before we even consider how many planets there might be. Speed is another concept that it can be difficult to grasp. We all know that the Earth moves in orbit around the Sun – and that the Sun is just one star in our galaxy. We may not know that our galaxy is moving at approximately one hundred million miles per hour towards a super-cluster known as the 'Great Attractor' – the centre of which is in the region of two hundred million light years away. This super-cluster, again only one of many, contains tens of thousands of galaxies.

This book is not about the Universe and my mind is not able – though yours may be – to fully understand the multitude of theories about the Big Bang, Dark Matter and Black Holes. I accept the fact that time and speed are related and that time travel is therefore theoretically possible, however, I find it difficult to comprehend how the restrictions of being unable to move faster than the ultimate velocity of light – might be overcome by taking short-cuts through Space via Worm-holes. Cosmology is not an easy subject for the layman. I include these last paragraphs only to put puny man in context with our known inorganic surroundings. Of course, there may be millions of other organic worlds out there. If there are many trillions of planets – as there must be – some must fall into the wonderfully named 'Goldilocks' category. These are the ones which, like baby bear's porridge, are 'just right' with the aquatic conditions for the creation and support of life. The chance of our planet being unique is a non starter. We have only fairly recently been able to detect planets outside our own solar system. It seems likely that within the foreseeable future, that the hundred scientists at the SETI (Search for Extraterrestrial Intelligence) institute in California will be twisting the wires off the Champagne corks.

Chapter Seven

CREATION OR CAUSAL DETERMINISM

With the help of the moon goddess, Tupa – the chief god of creation – landed on a hill in Paraguay and fashioned a male and a female figure out of clay. He then breathed life into them. They were Rupave, the 'Father of all People' and Sypave, the 'Mother of all People'. They were of the Guarani race – and it is from their children that all other races of the world descend.

This is the story of creation that is still passed down to many Paraguayan children, although Roman Catholicism took over as the country's main religion some centuries ago. Today, this landlocked and little known South American nation has a very homogeneous population. Over ninety per-cent of its people are of mixed race. They are descended from Spanish soldiers or male settlers and Guarani Indian women and, emanating from contrasting backgrounds, give Paraguay a rich culture. The official languages of the country are both Guarani and Spanish. A third tongue called Jopara, being an evolved mixture of the other two, is also widely used.

There are many thousands of folk legends, explaining how humans arrived on Earth. These can be found in all corners of the globe. They are not only confined to obscure tribes but form part of the teaching of major world religions. It would therefore be disrespectful of me to discount them. Although – for me – the idea is far less possible than unlikely, I have to agree that a very large number of people (even in the western culture I inhabit) are of the opinion that human beings are not part of the animal world. They believe that our ancestors arrived here, perhaps primitive but fully formed, spontaneously by the act of a supernatural creator. Exactly why this should be on the planet Earth, in such an infinite universe, is not usually explained. I will concede that a test-run might answer that question.

I don't know if I can satisfactorily explain this. All I can ask is that you think deeply about it. If human-kind had arrived here in the way many religions suggest, at the first moment 'after' our arrival we would still be bound by the same natural laws – which I have tried to explain in previous chapters. I accept that at the very moment of our appearance – which was even then subject to and modified by every influence outside ourselves – we could have free will. But at the next moment – and every subsequent fraction of time – we would be subject to the all-embracing conditions of what had gone before. Humans, like every other form of life, are unable to determine the future. The same natural laws would apply if we evolved (as I'm sure we did) or if a god created us.

There is another scenario that, like Jopara, has evolved from an unlikely matrimony – the union of science and religion. This, third way, is especially popular with theologians who enjoy scientific thought and some scientists who continue to subscribe to one of the world's religions. The third way accepts the evolutionary story, as I have outlined in this book, but believes that human beings are an exception to the rest of the animal kingdom. It suggests that at some juncture in our evolvement – perhaps when our brains had grown large enough – we were, either 'given' free will by being touched with a magic wand by the supreme deity, or alternatively that self-determination evolved naturally during the course of our emergence. Logic – for me – dismisses both suggestions. The gift from a god goes back to the creation idea and natural evolution must be a contradiction. The one thing that cannot evolve is free will.

Some people say that all animals have self determination. I must admit there have been times – on my 'normal' plane – when this has seemed so to me. I have a wonderful little dog called Blossom. As she came from a rescue centre I don't know her antecedents – although she looks (and acts) like a Tibetan terrier. She is a wonderfully affectionate and good dog who answers to her name and the word 'come'. However occasionally, when we go for a walk in the country, she will put on a spectacular display of disobedience. Blossom will run into a field and make no response when she is called. She might be sitting, looking at me (with a smile on her face?) and can hear me – yet the order 'come' makes no difference. Is she exhibiting free will, or is she just being contrary as there is a smell of rabbit in the air? I'm sure other dog owners have similar stories. It seems likely that all animals have some limited form of consciousness. Certainly those that have memories have experienced cultural evolution – as well as biological changes – in the same way as us. For those who 'believe' that free will evolved in man, I would like to ask at what stage in our pre-history did this occur?

I have another thought. Here I don't think that I am able to explain my mind processes in language, so can only suggest you give the idea long and hard consideration. Some of you may reach the same conclusion as myself. Try to consider what might happen if human self-determination was possible. That is, what would happen if individuals could step out and above from what had made them and what had gone before. What if they were able to act – as it were – out of the air? The answer, in my mind, is that long ago we would have ceased to exist. Having our actions restrained by our past, is not only logical, it is the only reason we are still here.

The great Ecclesiastes thinker, who told us that 'all is vanity', also wrote *there is no new thing under the sun*. As I suggested at the start of my reflections, many philosophers must have previously discussed the ideas that I have put forward here. As I only discovered their existence after I had already written part of this book, I have avoided reading anything they have to say. This was in the hope that new ideas would not influence the thoughts that had been in my mind for many years. When this book is published (if it is), I may try to read some of what they have written. However if I meet some heavy abstract jargon, I may be unable to follow their reasoning. I know I will be lost completely if their ideas are turned into mathematical equations. You may find that what I have written here is far too simplistic – but there would be little point in putting it together if some people were not able to grasp what I needed to say.

All philosophical ideas must have a title. This one is termed *Causal Determinism* or sometimes *Hard Determinism*. I'm not sure if this is a well chosen name as it seems too close to 'predestination', which is certainly not what I am trying to suggest. I am simply stating that, the first rule of life (as distinct from inert matter) is that it can only change from the influence of what has gone before – together with external pressure at that time. If this is so – as it must be – by extension, human free will cannot be possible. Some philosophers advocate *Soft Determinism,* which proposes that although the main thrust of our lives is determined by previous experiences, the minutiae is ours to decide. To me this is akin to eating your cake and still holding it in your hand. This suggestion must be completely illogical as there can be no demarcation between what is trivial and what is not.

The word 'belief' is frequently used in connection with religion, where it usually means unconditional acceptance of what someone has written or spoken. I therefore prefer the word conviction, to express the truths that I have come to regard as logical in my mind. If you have found these sketchy thoughts of mine interesting, you may ask if my convictions about free will have had any effect on the way I live my life. The answer is yes, they must have, yet much of the time I inhabit and enjoy the same emotional life as everyone who 'believes' they control their own destiny. I also react, initially at least, in the same way as other people. If I dine out and am presented with a poorly prepared meal, I might even complain – although I 'know' it is nobody's 'fault'. Like everyone else I have days when I am slightly depressed, but this has more to do with whether the sun is shining than too much deep contemplation. For the most part I enjoy living. Many of the chance occurrences of my life – so far – have been positive. If I – by chance – accepted the idea of God and his angels, I would consider I had a guardian one as I am usually lucky.

Those of us, who dwell in this contemporary 'western' civilization, find it extremely difficult to picture ourselves as biological creatures. It is not easy to strip ourselves completely from the incredibly rich emotional and cultural world that we inhabit.

Let us consider the experience of reading a few verses of profound poetry or, perhaps, a novel with some new deep insight of self revelation – or having tears brought to our eyes while listening to a section of emotive music, either by a great composer or maybe sung by a blackbird after a rainstorm. We may think about the mental intensity that can be gained after gazing at a painting or sculpture by a renowned artist, or the excitement and satisfaction that can be obtained both during and after the acquisition of knowledge – and for many people, I accept, the contentment, joy and completeness that a deep religious belief gives them. From these delights of the mind, to the more personal pleasures of relationships with other people, family members, friends, new acquaintances and even animal pets to the more carnal gratifications of good food, wine and sex – all seem important parts of our existence. Even more important is the physical wonder of just being alive and inside our own bodies, feeling the sun on our backs, the wind in our faces and breathing the air. All this, and so very much more, is what being human seems to us to be about.

Yet many of these centre-points of our existence are comparatively recent. Much of the literature, music and art that we enjoy – and that not only encompasses but also interprets many of the other aspects of our lives – has only evolved in the last five hundred years. The Christian religion only started two thousand years ago, the Moslem faith much more recently than that. I appreciate that the joy of being alive and personal relationships (and I guess blackbirds singing) goes back much further in time, but the point I am trying to make is that much of the 'clothing' of our lives today is relatively new. The exhilaration (for some) of watching their favourite football team or simple pleasure (for me) of chatting with friends, while having a pint in the pub, is extremely young.

All this is only true of our 'western' lives. Millions of humans in the world today inhabit a cultural evolvement much more sparse than ours. Life for them is still governed by fear. Pain, sickness, starvation and the struggle to live at all still dominates much of their time from their birth – as it did for our own ancestors not so very long ago. Many millions more live in cultures that are as rich as our own but, for reasons of historic chance, spend their lifetimes in an unremitting cycle of hopelessness and poverty if not in the anxiety of violence and terror. We now have almost only one thing in common with these groups – the great leveller itself.

If we are able to grasp that our cultural evolution is just that, that death is the unifying factor between us and every other living organism, perhaps we can mentally strip ourselves of all our clothing. We may then be able to see that indeed 'all is vanity' and that we have no more control over our lives than grass.

POSTSCRIPT

In the preface, I promised that the book would be brief – and I wrote that I trusted the explanation of my understanding of logic would be simple to follow. I hope that has been so. I also recorded that, as I recognised I had so far not found anyone who agreed with me, it seemed probable that few were likely to accept what I would put down (as, like most people, I rarely get into deep psychological discussion with strangers or friends I may have been wrong here). The book will not change anyone's opinion. If you find you agree with my reasoning, you must have – more or less – come to this conclusion before reading it. I would be extremely pleased if this book creates some response and be delighted to receive emails from readers. If you think my convictions are codswallop, please tell me the flaws in my personal explanation of how two and two make four. If you agree with what I have written, any comments will be welcome. If you have arrived at this paragraph, I presume you have read this little book. Your reaction can only be *as it is*.

email address: *asitis7@btinternet.com*

BIBLIOGRAPHY

Out of Eden; Stephen Oppenheimer (Constable - London 2003)

Extinction (Evolution and the end of Man); Michael Boulter (Harper Collins – London 2002)

The Wisdom of Bones, Alan Walker and Pat Shipman (Weidenfeld & Nicolson – London 1996)

African Exodus, Chris Stringer and Robin Mckie (Jonathan Cape – London 1996)

River out of Eden, Richard Dawkins (Weidenfeld & Nicolson – London 1995)

The Neandertal Enigma, James Shreeve (William Morrow – New York 1995)

The Runaway Brain, Christopher Wills (Harper Collins – New York 1993)

The Neandertals, Eric Trinkaus and Pat Shipman (Jonathan Cape – London 1993)

Origins Reconsidered, Richard Leakey and Roger Lewin (Little, Brown & Company – London 1992)

Darwin, Adrian Desmond and James Moore (Michael Joseph – London 1991)

Paradigms Lost, John L Casti (William Morrow – New York 1989)

Elaine Morgan on the Aquatic Ape Hypothesis:

The Descent of Woman (1972)
The Aquatic Ape (1982)
The Scars of Evolution (1990)
The Descent of the Child (1994)
The Aquatic Ape Hypothesis (1997)

All published by Souvenir Press - London